CW01019633

CELTIC SPELLS

A Year in the Life of a Modern Welsh Witch

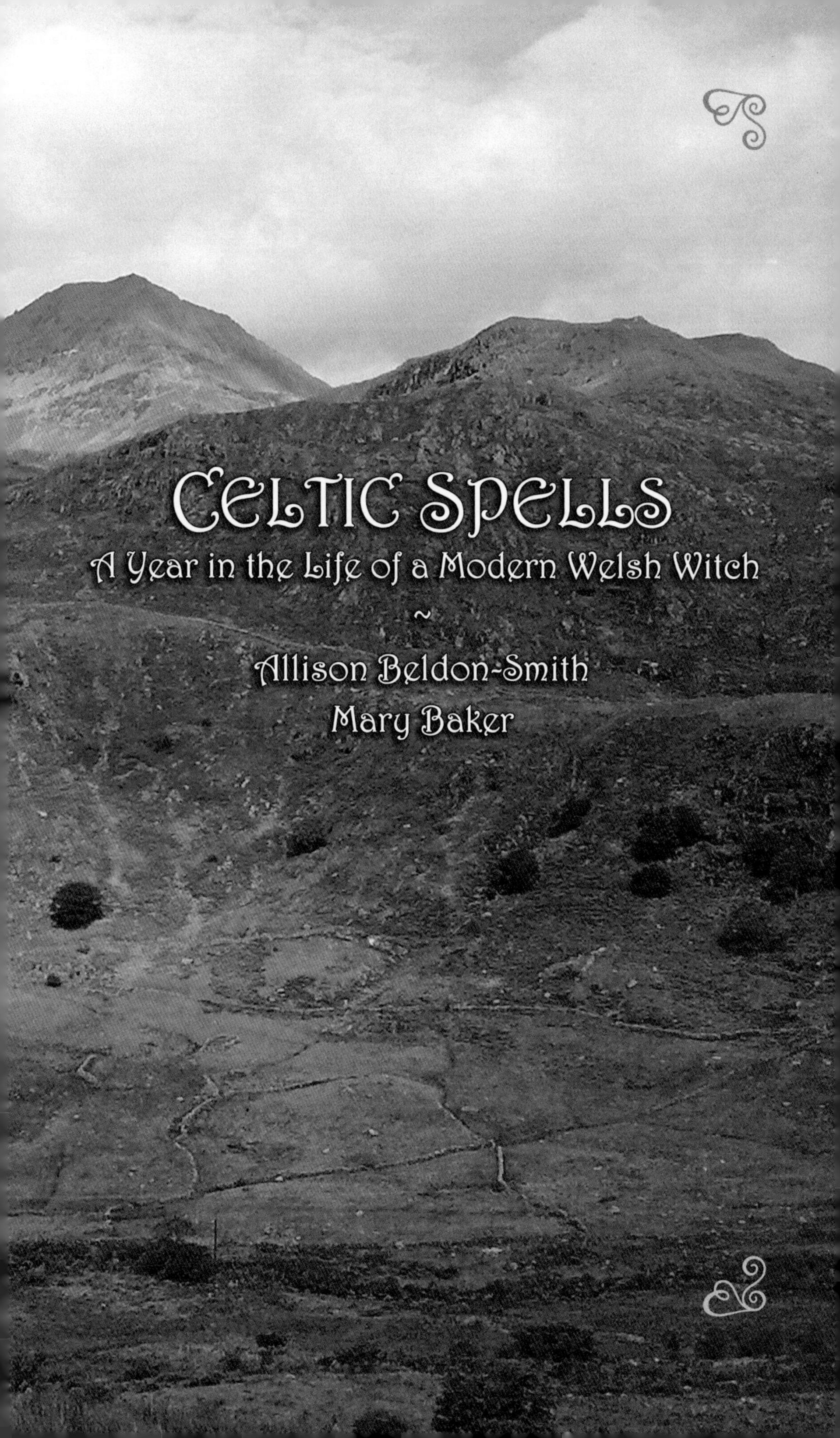

CELTIC SPELLS

A Year in the Life of a Modern Welsh Witch

~

Allison Beldon-Smith

Mary Baker

First published in the UK in 2013 by
Telos Publishing Ltd
17 Pendre Avenue, Prestatyn, Denbighshire LL19 9SH
www.telos.co.uk

Telos Publishing Ltd values feedback. Please e-mail us with any comments you may have about this book to: feedback@telos.co.uk

ISBN: 978-1-84583-083-0 (paperback)

Celtic Spells © 2013 Allison Beldon-Smith, Mary Baker

Photographic Credits:
Pages 6, 42, 48, 73, 81 and 87 © Marcus Beldon-Smith
Pages 10, 11, 12, 13, 51, 55, 62, 66, 88 © Stephanie de Gues
Page 8 © Anna Rankin
Page 34 © Frazer Hines
Page 95 © Marcus Bryan
All other photographs © Mary Baker

The moral right of the authors has been asserted.

Internal design, typesetting and layout by Paul Smith@Wonderful Books
www.wonderfulbook.co.uk

British Library Cataloguing in Publication Data.
A catalogue record for this book is available from the British Library.

This book is sold subject to the condition that it shall not by way of trade or otherwise, be lent, resold, hired out or otherwise circulated without the publisher's prior written consent in any form of binding or cover other than that in which it is published and without a similar condition including this condition being imposed on the subsequent purchaser.

WELCOME

I am Allison, and I am a witch. Here in Wales we have a tradition of calling people by their role and location rather than their name, hence I acquired the title of Talogwitch, the wise woman or seer of Talog, a beautiful hamlet here in Carmarthenshire.

I am also a Pagan Minister, a Seer, and an Earth Healer who, through the transition to cronehood, has realised it is time to teach rather than to do; time to pass on the knowledge to those who are willing to listen.

And this is where this little book comes in.

I live in the Welsh countryside with two black cats and a black dog, not forgetting a squealing pig (not for the pot this one).

My year is as yours, but ends as in ancient times, at Samhain, and begins anew on 1 November. But this volume follows the established Julian tradition, beginning in January and ending in December.

I love and appreciate nature, and trees, plants, stones and water all play an important role in my life. The four seasons influence the plants I use to heal, the spells I cast and my perception of the world around me.

This volume shares some of my knowledge and just a few of my many spells, that will hopefully give even the jaded city dweller a chance to reflect on the bounties of the Welsh countryside, the turning of the year's wheel and the changing nature of the seasons.

By bringing nature into your home, and embracing the bounty that she brings, your lives will be enriched, happier and more content.

So enjoy my thoughts, my words and my charms, and take away some of the happiness which I am freely sharing.

Bright Blessings,

Allison, Talogwitch

NEW
YEAR

JANUARY

This is a bleak cold month of meagre resources.
A time to hibernate, using inner resources to sustain.
It is a time for firelight families, stories and myths;
the passing on of ancient wisdom from the old to the young.

This is a busy and productive month as we look to recycle and re-purpose within the home, keeping busy while the weather is hostile. Here are five useful January spells to help positivity endure as we wait for the sun to return.

WEEK 1

WITCHES' WISHES

In scraps of material place the ingredients, then tie with string. Chant the spell three times.

LOVE ~ Pink Material
Thorn; rose hips / hawthorn berries
Spell: "Find me a partner who is true,
in total love I trust in you."

WEALTH ~ Green Material
Peach stone / orange pips; cloves
Spell: "For need not greed,
send me prosperity."

HEALTH ~ Blue Material
Sea shells / white quartz / flint; pine needles; bay leaf
Spell: "Heal, help and mend,
health endure until the end."

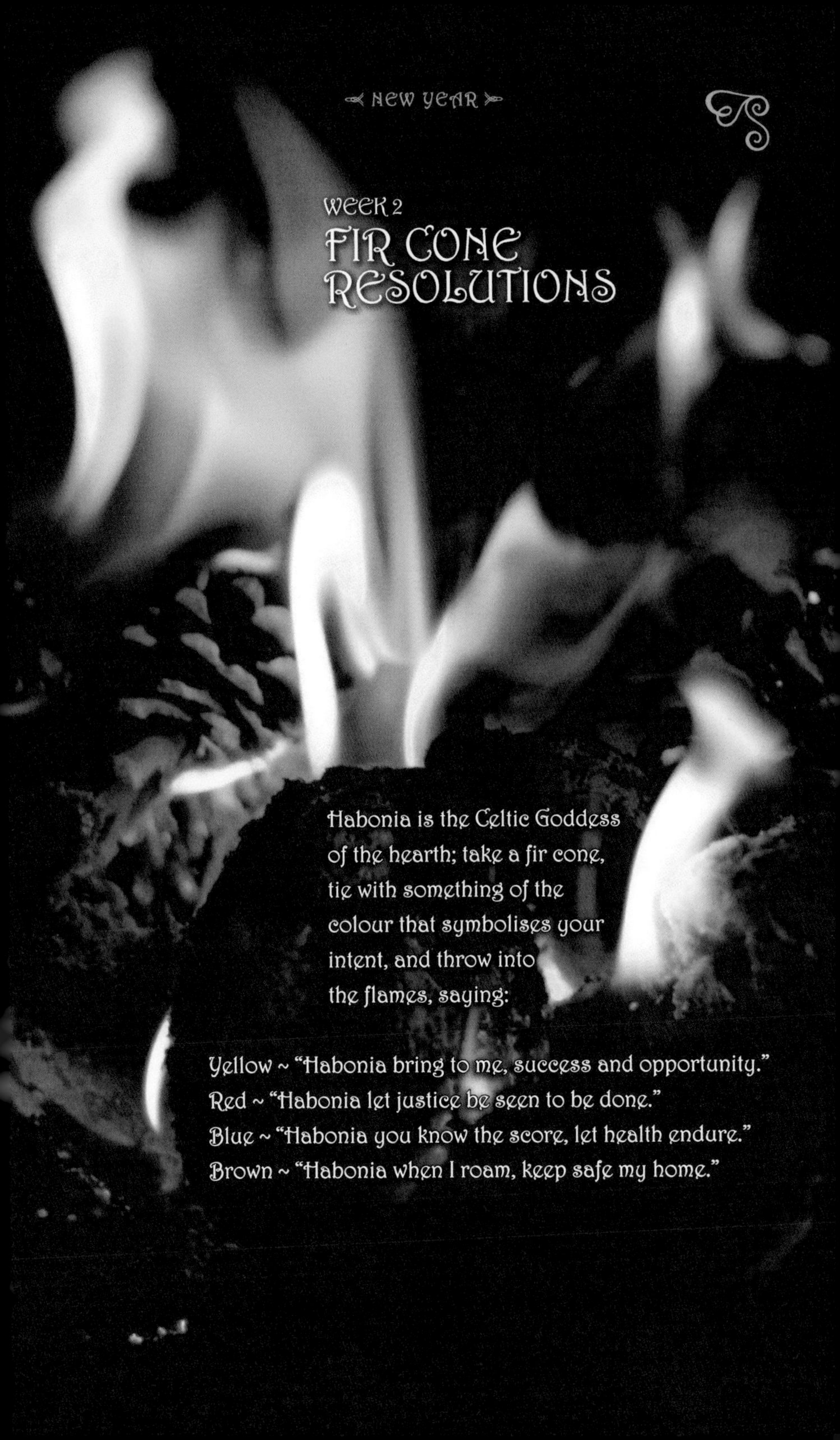

WEEK 2

FIR CONE RESOLUTIONS

Habonia is the Celtic Goddess of the hearth; take a fir cone, tie with something of the colour that symbolises your intent, and throw into the flames, saying:

Yellow ~ "Habonia bring to me, success and opportunity."
Red ~ "Habonia let justice be seen to be done."
Blue ~ "Habonia you know the score, let health endure."
Brown ~ "Habonia when I roam, keep safe my home."

WEEK 3

HOLLY WAND

Celts saw the holly bush as King of Winter,
a wood of great masculine passion and intent.

Take a cutting of holly wood,
and speak the Spell while holding it.

Spell of Intent (for urgent matters)
~ say during a Full Moon.

"Holly listen of what I speak
Urgently your help I seek;
May the future now be bent
By the power of my intent."

WEEK 4
PROSPERITY CANDLE

In ancient times, fire was the embodiment of hope; hence candles were not merely light givers but also symbolic of divine benevolence. Have a family meal by candlelight (one large candle in the centre); each person takes a coin, holds the edge in the flame till hot then presses it into the candle saying:

"May we never thirst, may we never hunger."

The candle is then placed over the fireplace and burned when times are dire.

WEEK 5

FIRE DIVINATION

Ask Habonia, Goddess of the Hearth,
for a glimpse of things to come.
Turn off all electrical devices, then sit by
an open fire, thinking of your question;
when ready throw dry holly on to the hot
embers, the fire will suddenly flourish with
fierce flame, see the fire sprites dance
forming pictures; 'read' the flames.

Keep a journal and
record your visions.

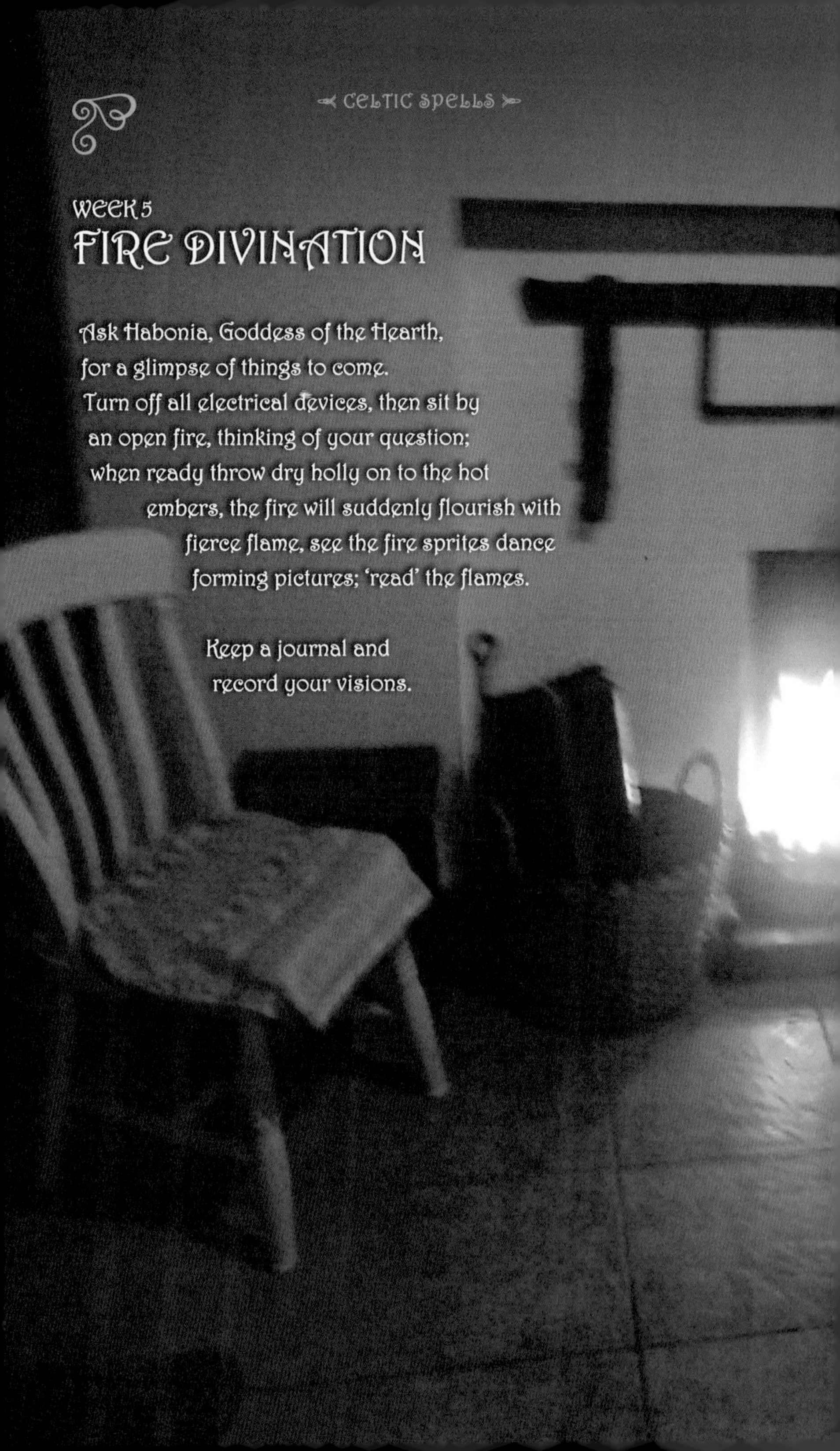

FEBRUARY

Imbolic is a harsh month when spirits need lifting and minds cleansing, for it is easy to slip into despair. The determined green of snowdrop lifts the gloom, though ice and frost may linger; days are starting to get longer.

The modern month for lovers, in reality February sees the spring child stirring in the womb of Mother Earth as we wait on the edge of a new season.

Spells this month include magic for self cleansing and spring cleaning, begining with self before tackling the house.

WEEK 6

BRIGIT CROSS

Traditionally made with long grass,
divide the bundle into four,
and secure each firmly.
Bend each to make a 'hook'.
Assemble by alternately crossing
under and over, and securing
the hooks back on self.

While making your cross chant:

"Burn fires burn,
turn wheel turn."

WEEK 7

FAERY HELP

While working, cleaning and doing chores, chant:

"Children of the Fey,
Show the way.
With me stay,
And help me."

WEEK 8

PSYCHIC SPRING CLEANING

Starting the highest point, go into every room of the house, sprinkling a few grains of salt into every corner and saying:

"Salt of the Earth cleanse this room for me,
Be gone all negativity."

End at the front door, open it and say:

"Be gone all negativity, you are unwanted, uninvited, do not return."

Then close the door.

WEEK 9

SELF CLEANSING

On a tray place a candle, a bowl of sea salt and a larger bowl of rain water. Put a pinch of salt into the water, stirring with your fingers, saying:

"Into your keeping,
Mother, I put my
fears and worries."

Now list all that worries you, totally unburdening yourself. Then say:

"It's done,
they are gone,
May I now
move on."

Take the bowl of water to the toilet and flush your troubles away.

SPRING

MARCH

Perhaps a time to indulge a little madness. Certainly a time for the good intentions promised earlier to begin in earnest. Cobwebs need clearing, drawers need sorting, as do our lives. The hare runs free reminding us that we too should reaffirm our freedom, shaking loose any shackles that life is trying to impose.

Rituals for March are of self empowerment through knowledge and loving acceptance.

Wild yellow daffodils grace our Welsh lanes, magnificent in their individuality, reminding us that there is nothing more precious than freedom.

WEEK 10

SELF ACCEPTANCE RITUAL

You require Rose petals steeped in sunflower oil.
Anoint self with the oil, saying:

"Mother I embrace your blessed air,
I breathe, I live, I am.
Mother I embrace your blessed fire,
cleansed by flame, in my simplicity I am.
Mother embracing your blessed water,
as blood within, you made me thus, I am.
Mother I embrace earth, thankful for my existence,
here and now, just as I am."

WEEK 11

DAWN SALUTE

Catch the dawn, or as early as you can, face the rising sun saying:

"Air inspire,
Within me, burn fire,
Rain upon me water,
Earth embrace your daughter.
Awake now the Amazon in me,
Make me the best that I can be."

Now, raising your arms up, fill your lungs and let out a mighty roar.

WEEK 12

BREAK THE SHACKLES

The Seven Faces are unseen cultural shackles:
Assumption, Deceit, Denial, Envy,
Expectation, Greed and Guilt.

You need a jar and seven different seeds or nuts,
one for each of the Faces.
For example: split pea, corn, pumpkin, sunflower,
peanut, lentil and barley.
Ensure that what you choose is bird-friendly.

From day one,
every time you find you have to confront one of the Faces,
put that seed into the jar.

At the end of the week, your jar will contain a grand mixture.
Now scatter it for the birds.
Feel their freedom and know you have reclaimed yours.

WEEK 13

'COME SPRING COME' RITUAL

You need five candles of different colours.
Place in a compass square:
White (Goddess) in the centre;
Yellow (Air) to the East;
Red (Fire) to the South;
Blue (Water) to the West; and
Green (Earth) to the north.
Light the candles in turn, saying:

White ~ "Mother Earth hear my call, Awaken, return spring to all."
Yellow ~ "I am the dawn, all the potentiality of Spring; sunlight I bring."
Red ~ "I am the sun at noon, heat will return soon."
Blue ~ "I am the sun slipping away, breathing peace, ending day."
Green ~ "I am night bringing rest, day's end, forever blessed."

APRIL

April is a good time to use rain magic. Water replenishes and is a benevolent gift that brings rejoicing and celebration. Too often in our Western culture we see rain as an inconvenience rather than a gift. When rain falls one can almost hear nature growing.

This is a vibrant fresh month of newness and promise,

I use the energy of the water to bring a zing and newness to rituals of positivity, growth, opportunity and success.

WEEK 14

DAWN'S DEW SPELL

Rise at dawn and collect dew from the plants in a glass vessel. Return indoors and stir the dew with a silver spoon three x three times saying:

> "Dew at dawn, gifted free,
> By the power of three times three
> Bring prosperity to me."

Then anoint yourself with the dew on both the hands and forehead.

WEEK 15

HEALING RAIN

'April brings the showers' so the old rhyme says. On a nice typical wet day, step out on three separate occasions into the downpour and let Gaia's tears wash over you. On each embrace of nature turn three full clockwise revolutions while saying three times:

"Gaia's tears, falling rain,
Heal me, make me well again.
By the power of three times three,
As I will, so mote it be."

WEEK 16

OSTARA RAINBOWS

Bring rainbows into your home. Put food colouring in the water when you boil eggs, or hand-paint them, to make a bowl of rainbow eggs for the table. Hang crystals at the windows bringing rainbows into the home every time the sun plays upon them. Tie ribbons of rainbow colours on your door handles and taps.

While you are decorating your home with colour, chant:

"Welcome Ostara,
Welcome the sun,
The wheel has turned,
Spring has sprung."

WEEK 17

GREEN TO GOLD SPELL

Pick seven yellow April flowers.
In numerology, seven is the number of protection;
and most of us could do with a little financial protection.
As you pick each individual flower say:

“Green to gold, Green to gold
Make me rich before I'm old.’

Place them in a vase facing north, saying:

“Green to gold, Green to gold
Make me rich before I'm old,
Not for opulence, not for greed
But to pay the bills and for things I need.”

MAY

In May there is a freshness and energy as the lush green leaves adorn our newly clothed trees. The sun gives heat that warms our faces and allows us to shed our winter clothing. May Queens, May poles and Morris dancers are still in evidence, appearing at this time of Beltane and linking us with times and beliefs from the distant past. The bluebell spreads its gorgeous carpet in woodland shade, oozing a sweet heavy perfume that entwines with the exotic scent of wild garlic.

WEEK 18

BELTANE SALUTE

May is the lusty month of fun and frolic, and, above all, knowing what we want. It is time to personally welcome Mother Earth. Walk your home boundary scattering birdseed to encircle your property. As you walk, communicate intent with your chosen number of steps, interspaced with a small jump.

"Come walk upon hallowed ground,
Summer beckons all around,
Welcome Beltane with leap and bound."

Choose the number of steps:

3 = opportunity, change;
5 = enchantment;
7 = protection;
9 = enlightenment
and perfection.

WEEK 19

DAISY CHAIN MAGIC

Daisies grow everywhere, from lawns to hedgerows. Whether big or small, pick them with long stems, then slit and pass the other stem through, making a traditional chain.

As you gather them, say:

"Clean and new,
There's much to do."

Then, as you construct your chain, say repeatedly:

"I have need,
Mother heed ________"

replacing the blank with what you most need. For example: "I need money for heating oil."

WEEK 20

BELTANE BELLS

Beltane's bells hold special Fairy significance; this is why Morris dancers are decked in them.

Make a Beltane Plait to hang at the door. Take three lengths of ribbon"

~ Blue (Health)
~ Green (Wealth)
~ Purple (Wise)

and 13 tiny bells. As you plait, include the bells on the ribbons, saying:

"May summer days be long and fine,
Strength, abundance and wisdom be mine."

Now hang the plait on the door; every time it jingles it will remind you.

WEEK 21
MAY IS OUT

The flowering Hawthorn is called May Blossom. The old saying is: 'Don't cast a clout 'til May is out.' This is the time to change into summer clothing. Mats are taken out and given a good 'clout' to get the dust out. It is also symbolic of inner cleansing.

Hang your rug over the washing line and beat, saying:

"Give it a clout, clout, clout,
Everyone shout, shout, shout,
May it out, out, out."

WEEK 22

FAERY WISHES

Every village used to have an aged hawthorn tree, considered to be the portal to an 'Otherworld'. Faery wishes made when the hawthorn blossoms are considered especially magical.

Tie a coloured rag or ribbon in the branches, representing your intent; and leave a small gift in payment.

Yellow = Opportunity
Orange = Success
Pink = Love
Red = Justice
Purple = Wisdom
Blue = Health
Green = Plenty
Brown = Protection
White = Babies
Grey = Problems
Black = To take away something

Never remove anything that someone else has added to the tree.

SUMMER

JUNE

The Summer solstice brings the longest day; meadows are a colourful abundance of wild flowers. All of Nature is on the move, from the tiniest insect, through to fox and badger. Even to us, using the long hours of sunshine for drying blankets on the line and the picking and drying of herbs for spells and cooking.

WEEK 23

FRIENDSHIP SPELL

This can be done at any time. Just gather your friends and share a meal jointly prepared and cooked. Agree upon the dish ~ it needs to be one that is stirred like an old fashioned stew. Each friend brings an ingredient and, as it is added, they stir, saying:

"My love and truth, into the pot go,
That our friendship may grow."

When serving, pass the pot around and, as each takes their share, say:

"May we always be friends."

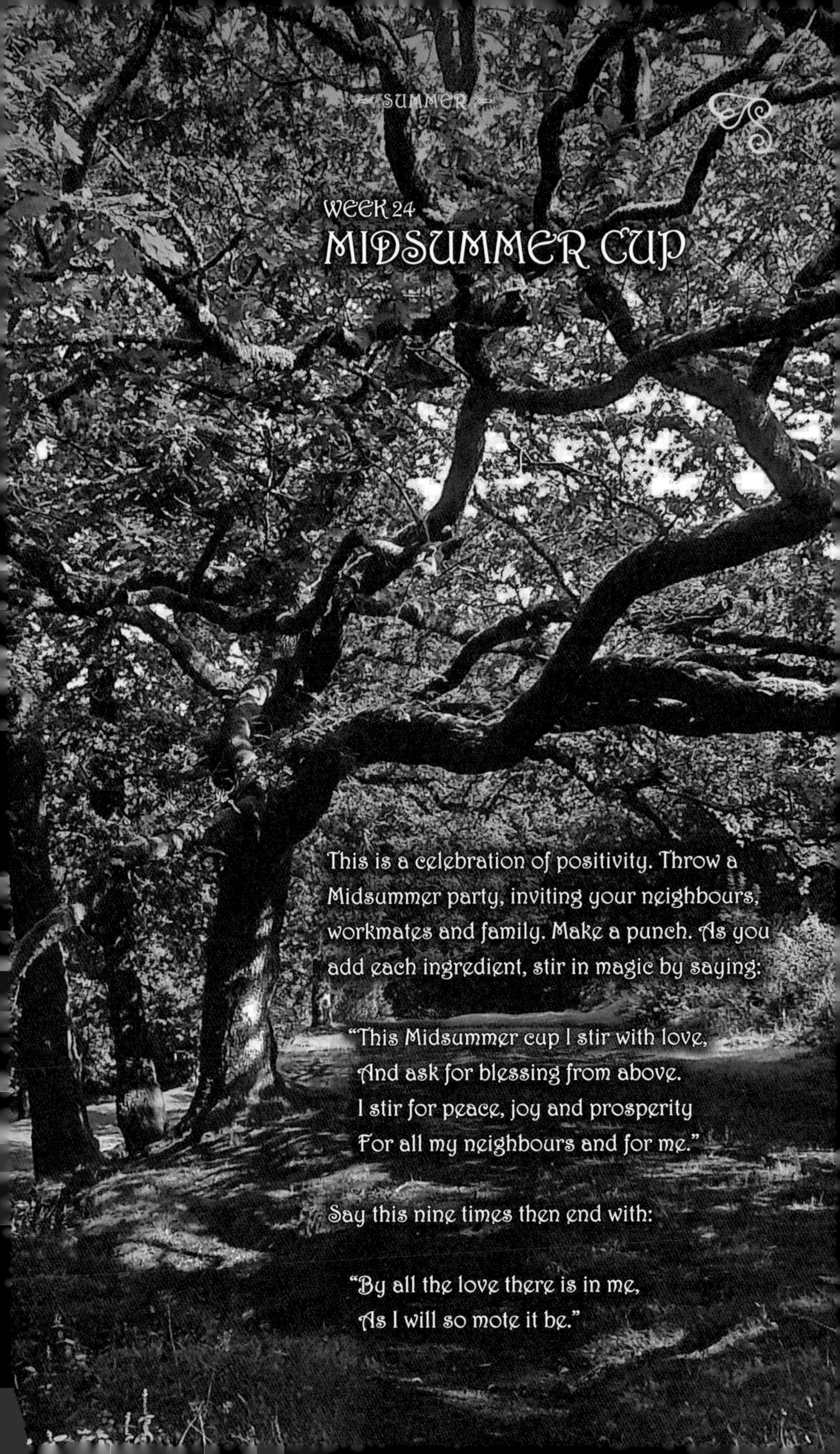

WEEK 24

MIDSUMMER CUP

This is a celebration of positivity. Throw a Midsummer party, inviting your neighbours, workmates and family. Make a punch. As you add each ingredient, stir in magic by saying:

"This Midsummer cup I stir with love,
And ask for blessing from above.
I stir for peace, joy and prosperity
For all my neighbours and for me."

Say this nine times then end with:

"By all the love there is in me,
As I will so mote it be."

WEEK 25

GOD'S EYE AMULET

Midsummer is the longest day. Sun energy is
masculine, manifesting as power and protection.
Now is the time to make your God's Eye.

Take two sticks of wood, 13 inches long, and a ball of wool.
Using the wool, tie the sticks centrally to make a cross,
then from this repeatedly wind the wool
over and under and around saying:

"Blue skies, longest day,
Sunshine keep the rain away."

Hang at the door for protection.

Next Midsummer, burn it and make another.

WEEK 26

LAVENDER CROSS

Lavender for the Celts has always been used for Love magic and as an aphrodisiac; it is often burned at handfastings.

A lavender cross is made by taking four equal bunches, each tied securely at either end, then woven together in the tradition of Celtic knotting, with alternate over and under, to form a cross. Further tie each point of crossing-over so that the central 'knot' is secure.

While you work say three times:

"Lavender's green, lavender's blue,
Send me a lover who will be true."

JULY

Butterflies, bees and all manner of insects fill the air, attending the hedgerows, visiting honeysuckle, wild thyme, woodbine, wild rose, and not forgetting the endless brambles! Busy birds sing their hearts out at the crack of dawn. Fruit, seed, and nuts are fattening; everything is growing. Rain comes between sunshine and thus we get many rainbows, everywhere is so lush and green. Dragonflies, like fairies, flitter on iridescent wings around the village pond and streams. Everywhere is alive.

WEEK 27
RAINBOW MAGIC

Rainbows are formed by refracted light off rain-drops. Bring this Goddess gift into your home by hanging crystals at an east-facing window.

Rainbows are known to be magical; light is the precious gift. It is wonderful to wake at dawn to a room dancing with faeries. As you lie in bed, salute them and let your spirit dance with them, saying:

"Rainbow faeries with your gift of light,
Make my day both happy and bright."

WEEK 28

HONEYSUCKLE PROTECTION SPELL

Honeysuckle was, for the Celts, symbolic of the journey home. This spell must be cast outside, for to bring Honeysuckle indoors is very unlucky.

It grows wild in the woods and hedgerows, and when in bloom can easily be seen. Cut a length approximately your height then wind it into a wreath, saying seven times:

> "Celtic labyrinth, life's journey home,
> Keep me safe, where 'ere I roam."

Hang the wreath in a tree close to your home.

WEEK 29

'STAY AWAY' SPELL

Summer is popular for weddings but it is also a time of partings.
This is a spell to be lovingly rid of someone who is being a nuisance.

Cut a length of young blackthorn and bend it into a wreath; anchor securely with red ribbon. Beware the thorns, they are sharp!
If you get pricked, then offer your blood as payment to the Fey.

Roll up a photograph of the culprit and attach it to the wreath, saying seven times:

"From unwanted attention set me free
Blackthorn keep ________ {name} away from me."

Hang the completed wreath over your door.

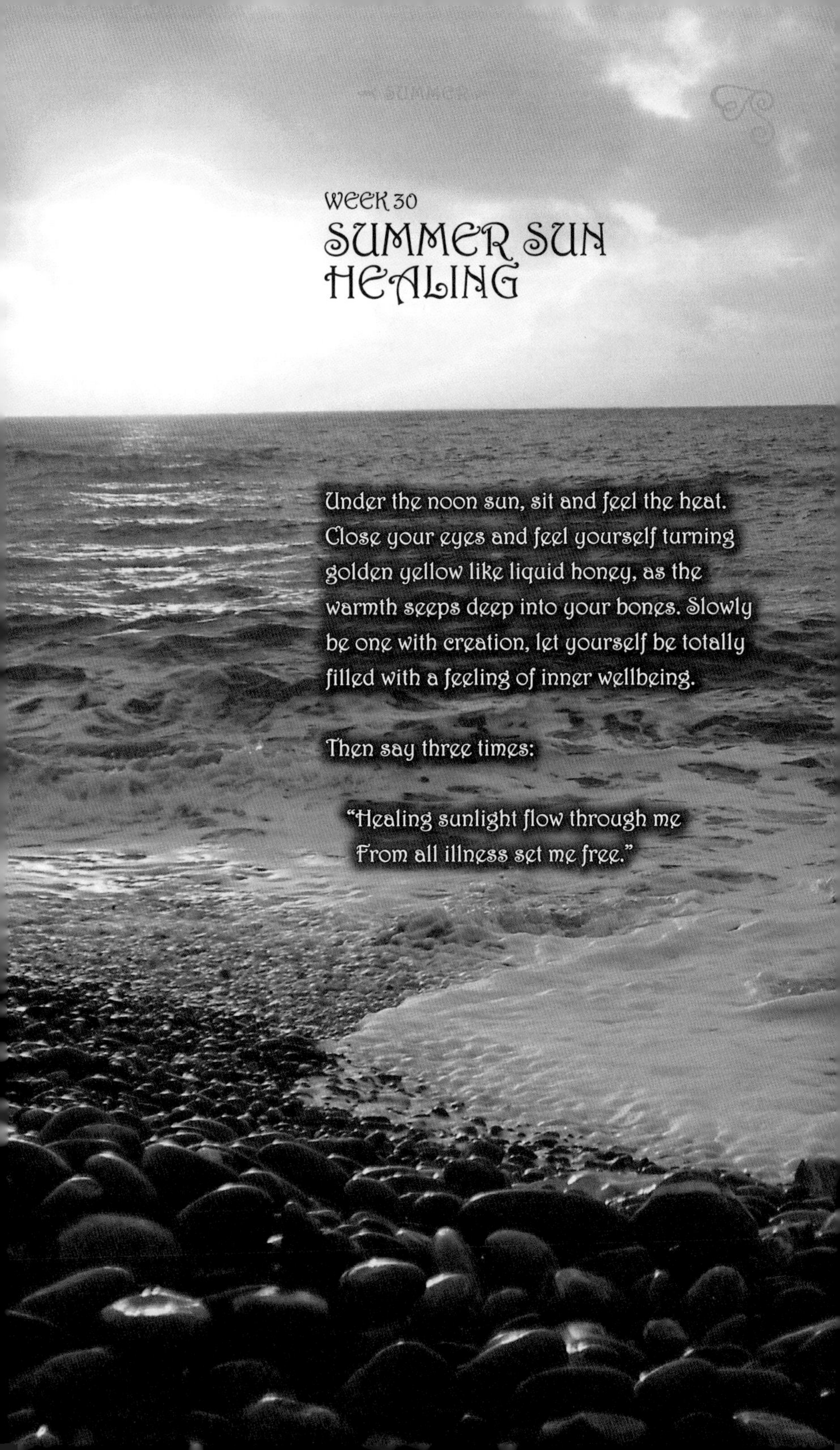

WEEK 30

SUMMER SUN HEALING

Under the noon sun, sit and feel the heat. Close your eyes and feel yourself turning golden yellow like liquid honey, as the warmth seeps deep into your bones. Slowly be one with creation, let yourself be totally filled with a feeling of inner wellbeing.

Then say three times:

"Healing sunlight flow through me
From all illness set me free."

AUGUST

A time of sunshine and travel, holidaymakers are drawn to the beaches and the sea. This is the time of the first harvest known as Lughnasadh. Fields are cut and crops harvested, orchards picked of fruit; from gardens and allotments nature's bounty is gathered. In the wild woodlands, the birds, insects and wildlife are also taking advantage of this time of plenty to eat and to grow strong.

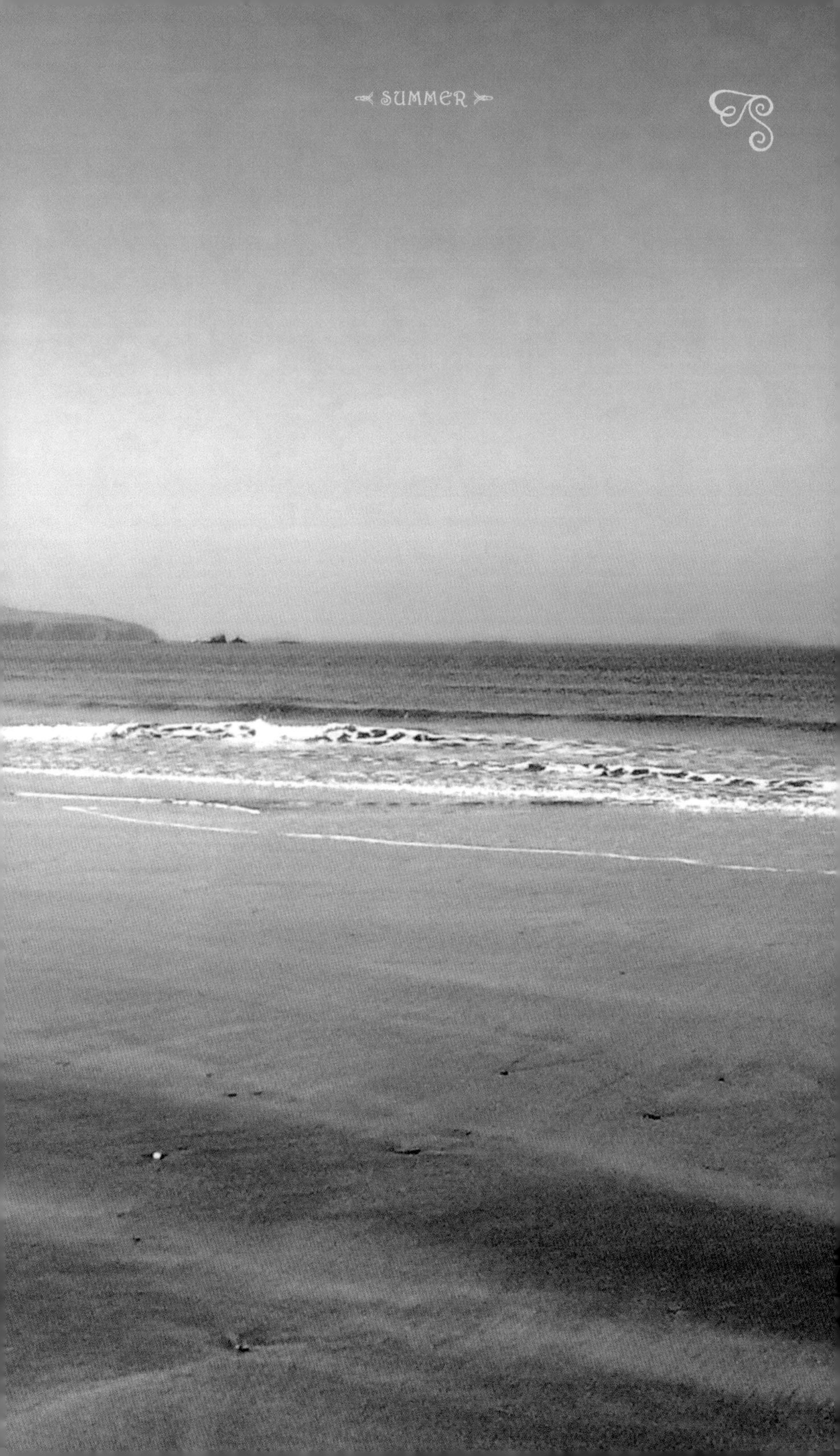

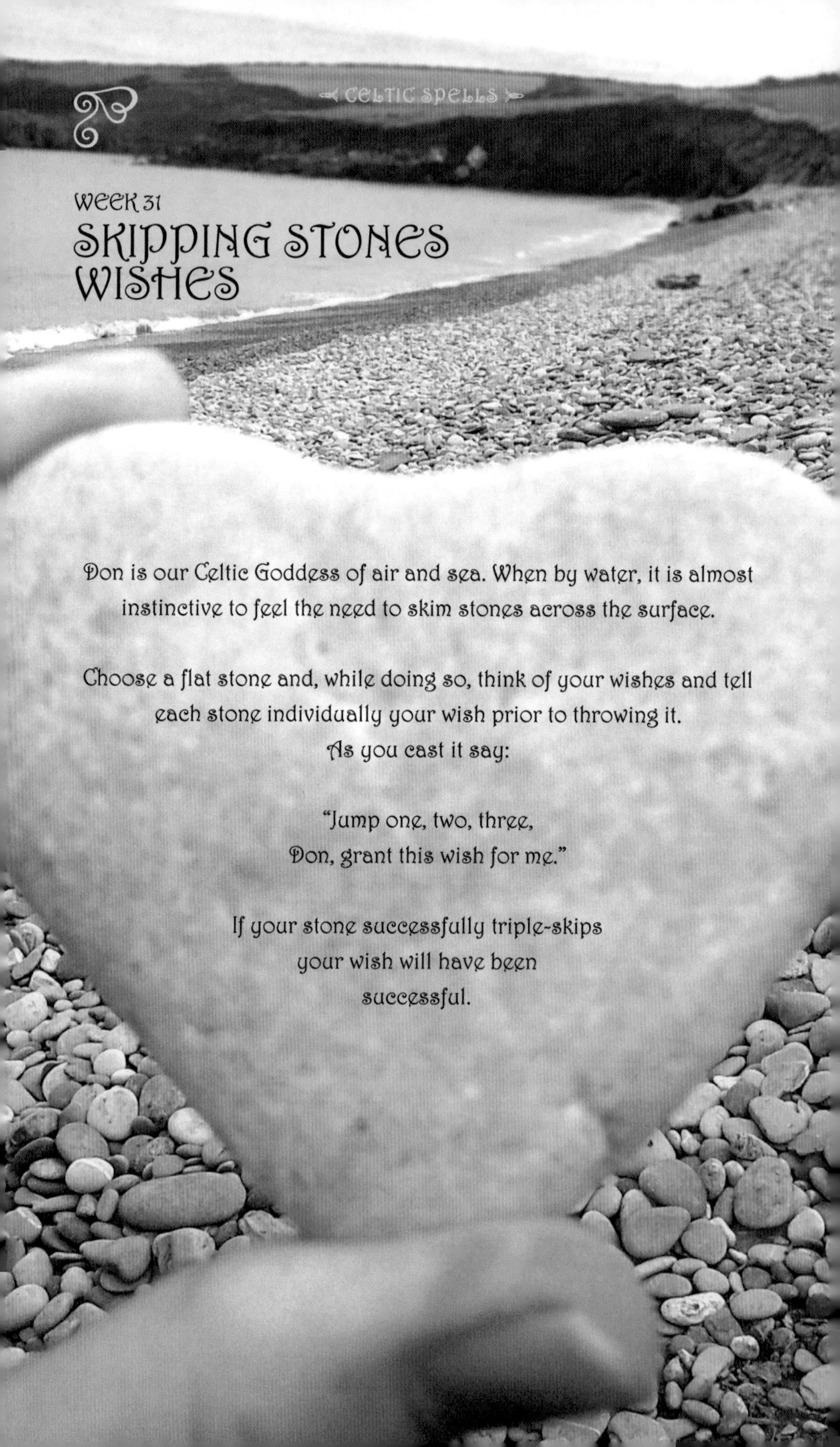

WEEK 31

SKIPPING STONES WISHES

Don is our Celtic Goddess of air and sea. When by water, it is almost instinctive to feel the need to skim stones across the surface.

Choose a flat stone and, while doing so, think of your wishes and tell each stone individually your wish prior to throwing it.
As you cast it say:

"Jump one, two, three,
Don, grant this wish for me."

If your stone successfully triple-skips
your wish will have been
successful.

WEEK 32

'PLENTY' SPELL

Rosmerta, the 'Great Provider', is the
Celtic Goddess of Fertility and Abundance.

Plait three long lengths of meadow grass.
As you plait, keep adding more into the lengths
so that they grow longer until
your plait can turn a nice circle.

Now cross the ends and anchor well.
Take a bright ribbon, wind it around the wreath
and tie in a bow.

As you work assembling the
wreath say nine times:

"Rosmerta bring plenty to me;
Bring me prosperity."

Hang at your door
for the sun to energize.

WEEK 33

ROSE PETAL WISHES

Roses by August are full blown and dropping their petals. Gather some and find some flowing water, a big lazy old river is best. Scatter the petals onto the water and, as you do this, speak your hopes to the Water Sprites, saying:

"Water, silent and deep you flow,
Well my lot in life you know;
Take my hopes and make then grow."

Then watch the petals float away into the wide world and blow them a kiss for luck.

WEEK 34

HAG STONE HUNTING

A Hag stone, or Glain Neidr, is a stone with a naturally occurring hole right through it.

Since the dawn of time the Glain Neidr has been seen as a gift from the Earth Mother, an amulet of protection, for it is one element surrounding another; earth encircling air.

As you search say:

"Goddess guide my eyes that I may see,
The Hag stone that is meant for me."

When you find one wear it or carry it with you.

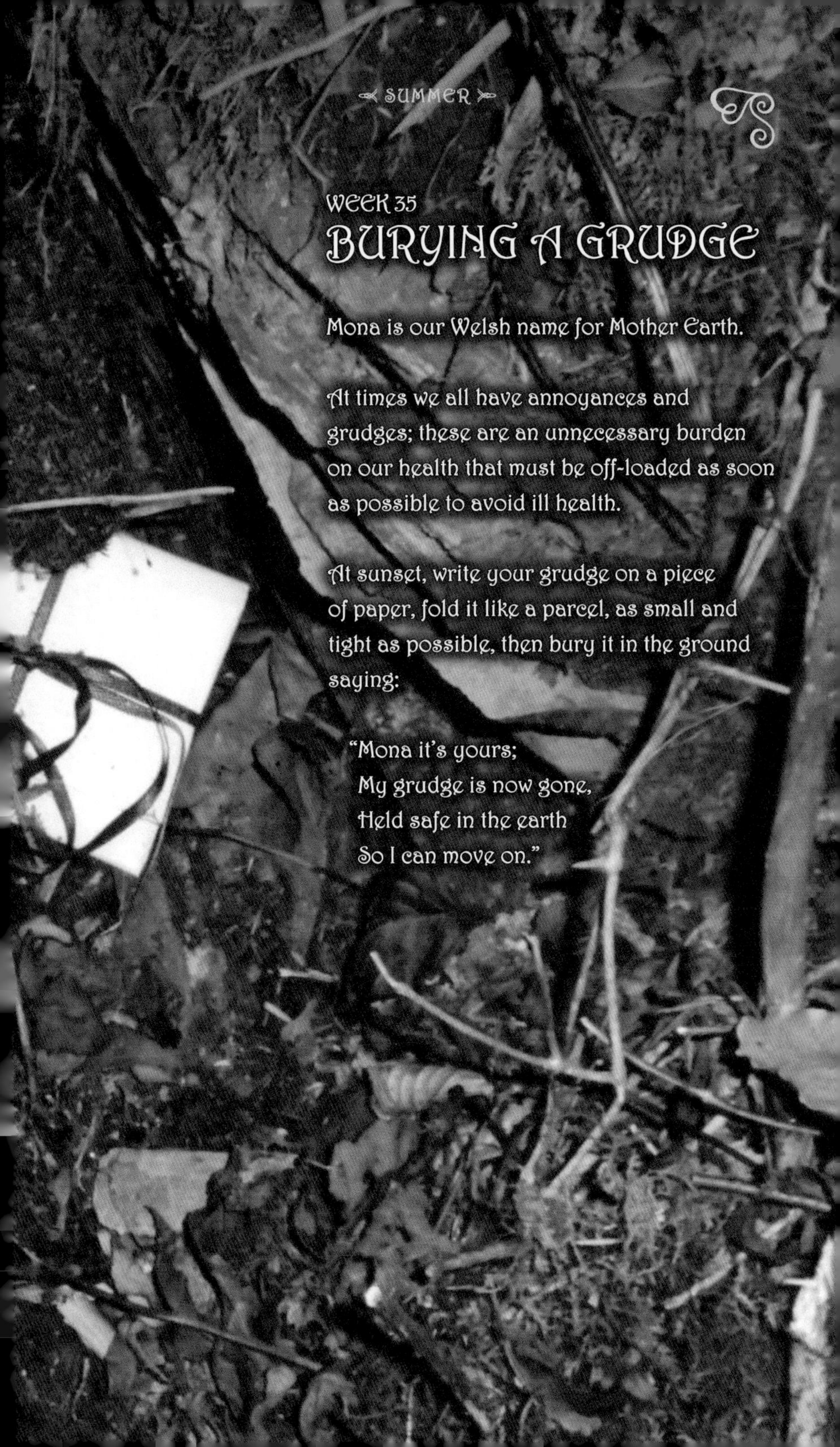

WEEK 35

BURYING A GRUDGE

Mona is our Welsh name for Mother Earth.

At times we all have annoyances and grudges; these are an unnecessary burden on our health that must be off-loaded as soon as possible to avoid ill health.

At sunset, write your grudge on a piece of paper, fold it like a parcel, as small and tight as possible, then bury it in the ground saying:

> "Mona it's yours;
> My grudge is now gone,
> Held safe in the earth
> So I can move on."

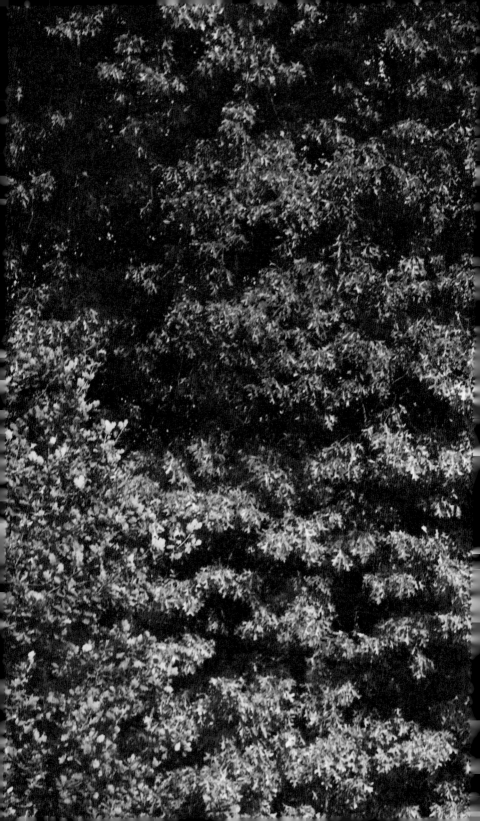

AUTUMN

SEPTEMBER

Back to school, and back to reality. The harvesting still continues, with the trees and bushes now laden with nuts, berries and seeds; squirrels are busy as are all woodland creatures, knowing the summer is drawing to a close and cold will soon return. We feel the chill in the air. Leaves start to show discolour heralding the time of Mabon, or Harvest Home, the Autumn equinox.

WEEK 36

CLAN MARK

This is fruit-picking time,
a job made easier when the whole tribe
participates, so make it interesting.

In the manner of Woad, mix a little blue food colouring with water. As a family, choose simple symbols ~ perhaps a spiral, moon, sun or star ~ then paint your chosen symbol on your cheek, forehead or collarbone.

Every 'hunting trip' mark your clan, saying:

"Mother of All, protect and keep
Bounteous harvest may we reap."

Then go forth and gather nature's harvest.

WEEK 37

CLOUD DIVINATION

Look at cloud formations; it is not necessary to put aside special time, just allow yourself to be drawn to cloud gazing when Arianrod, Goddess of the boundless skies, calls you.

Breathing deeply, be one with all creation, then say:

> "Goddess of the boundless skies
> Grant prophecy unto my eyes."

Now look deep into the cloud formations, what do you see?

Keep a diary and record your thoughts.

WEEK 38
LOOK THE DEVIL IN THE EYE

When a Witch says "look the devil in the eye", she means look inside yourself. If there is any negativity within, then more will draw to it, for 'like draws to like', and this is the essence of magic.

At night, take a mirror and a single candle, look deep into your own eyes and feel the strange energy that is generated; let mortal and immortal connect, then merge in perfect harmony. In total peace say:

"I banish all negativity,
May the Goddess live in me."

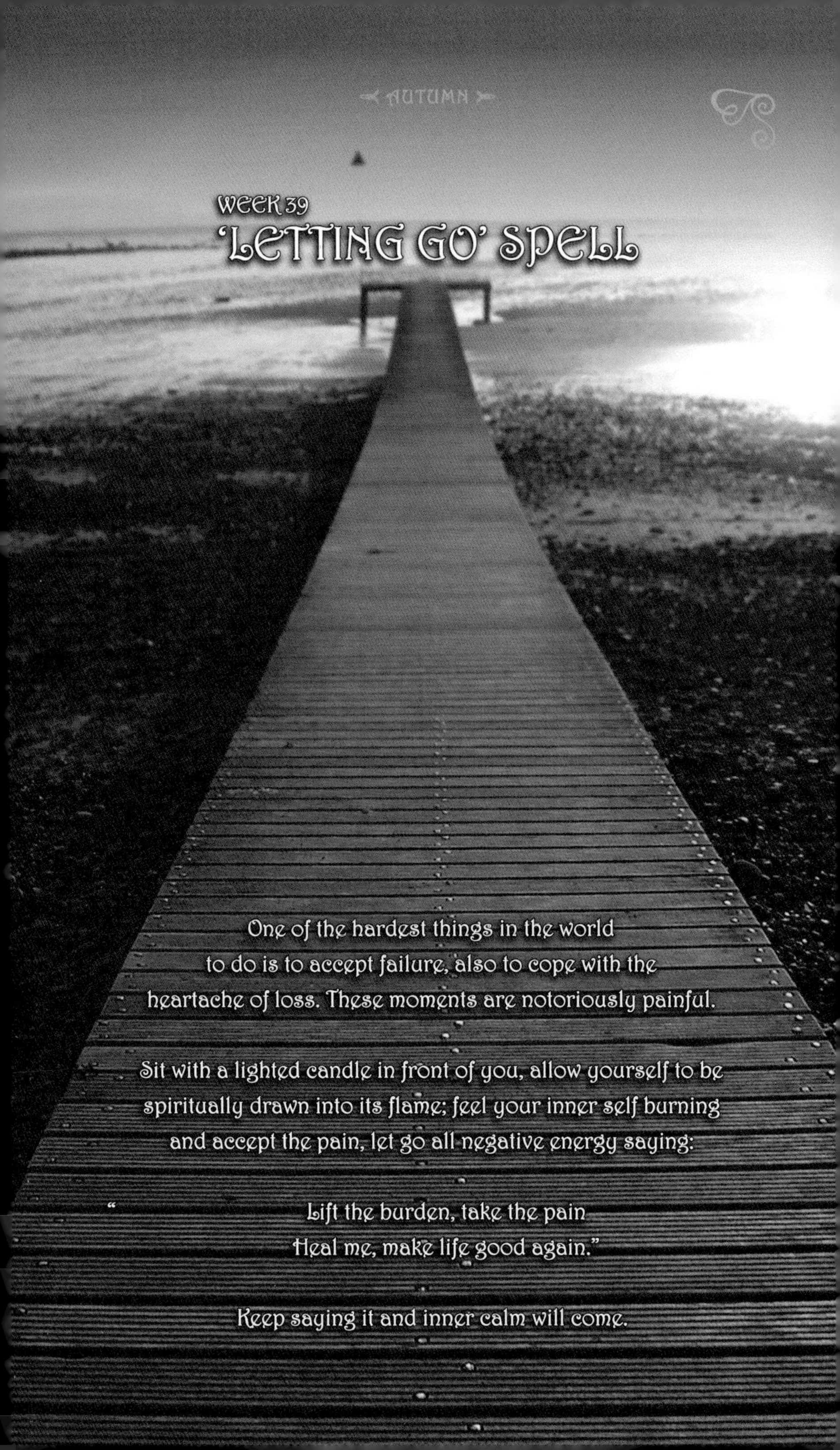

WEEK 39
'LETTING GO' SPELL

One of the hardest things in the world to do is to accept failure, also to cope with the heartache of loss. These moments are notoriously painful.

Sit with a lighted candle in front of you, allow yourself to be spiritually drawn into its flame; feel your inner self burning and accept the pain, let go all negative energy saying:

"Lift the burden, take the pain
Heal me, make life good again."

Keep saying it and inner calm will come.

OCTOBER

Samhain or Halloween, the end of the Celtic year, the time when the veil between this world and the spirit world is at its thinnest; a sombre time of remembering ancestors and departed loved ones, even talking to them; celebrating the joy of their lives by sharing and recalling within the family, fond memories of bygone days. Mother Nature's mantle turns from green to gold and then to brown, the winds blow and leaves fall; days grow short and nights draw in.

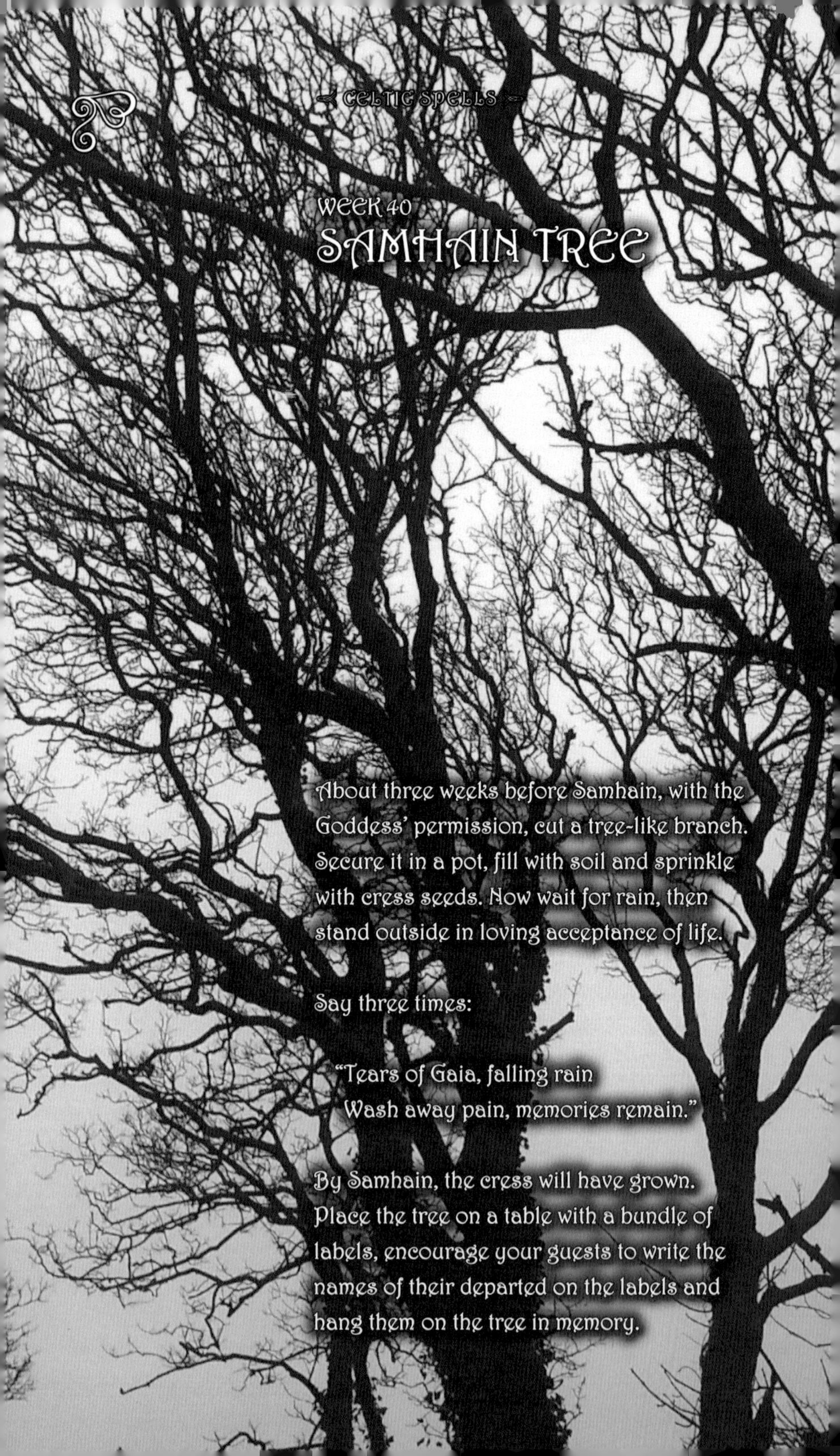

WEEK 40

SAMHAIN TREE

About three weeks before Samhain, with the Goddess' permission, cut a tree-like branch. Secure it in a pot, fill with soil and sprinkle with cress seeds. Now wait for rain, then stand outside in loving acceptance of life.

Say three times:

"Tears of Gaia, falling rain
Wash away pain, memories remain."

By Samhain, the cress will have grown. Place the tree on a table with a bundle of labels, encourage your guests to write the names of their departed on the labels and hang them on the tree in memory.

WEEK 41

BE PENTAGRAM

Stand under a moonlit sky. Stand and be one with creation. Turn clockwise slowly three times then declare your affiliation with the Goddess and the universe.

“My breath is Air,
My intent is Flame,
My blood is Water,
Earth is my frame,
Spirit is me,
Pentagram I be.’

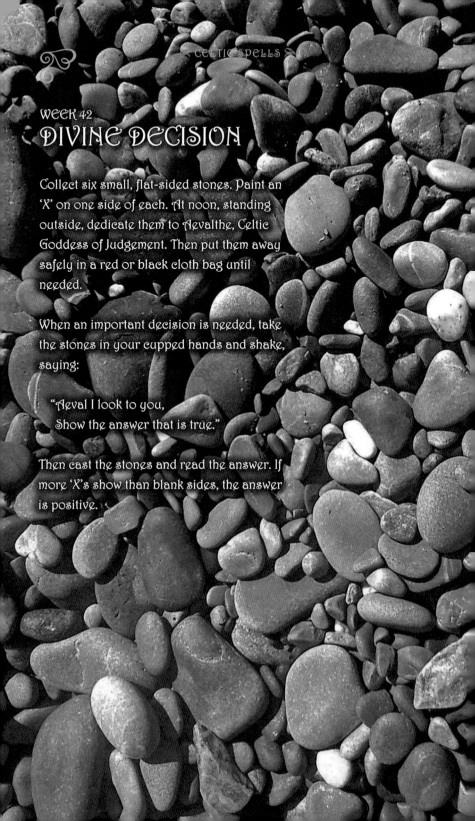

WEEK 42

DIVINE DECISION

Collect six small, flat-sided stones. Paint an 'X' on one side of each. At noon, standing outside, dedicate them to Aevalthe, Celtic Goddess of Judgement. Then put them away safely in a red or black cloth bag until needed.

When an important decision is needed, take the stones in your cupped hands and shake, saying:

"Aeval I look to you,
Show the answer that is true."

Then cast the stones and read the answer. If more 'X's show than blank sides, the answer is positive.

WEEK 43
WALK IN THE LIGHT

Many people fear the concept of Halloween as portrayed by Christian belief, which advises all spirit visitation to be negative. This is why Jack-o-Lanterns are made, to frighten away the evil spirits. But this notion is not true. The rule is simple: 'Like draws to like'.

For peace of mind say:

> "If you're good you can stay,
> If you're bad then go away!"

WEEK 44

SAMHAIN, ALL HALLOWS EVE

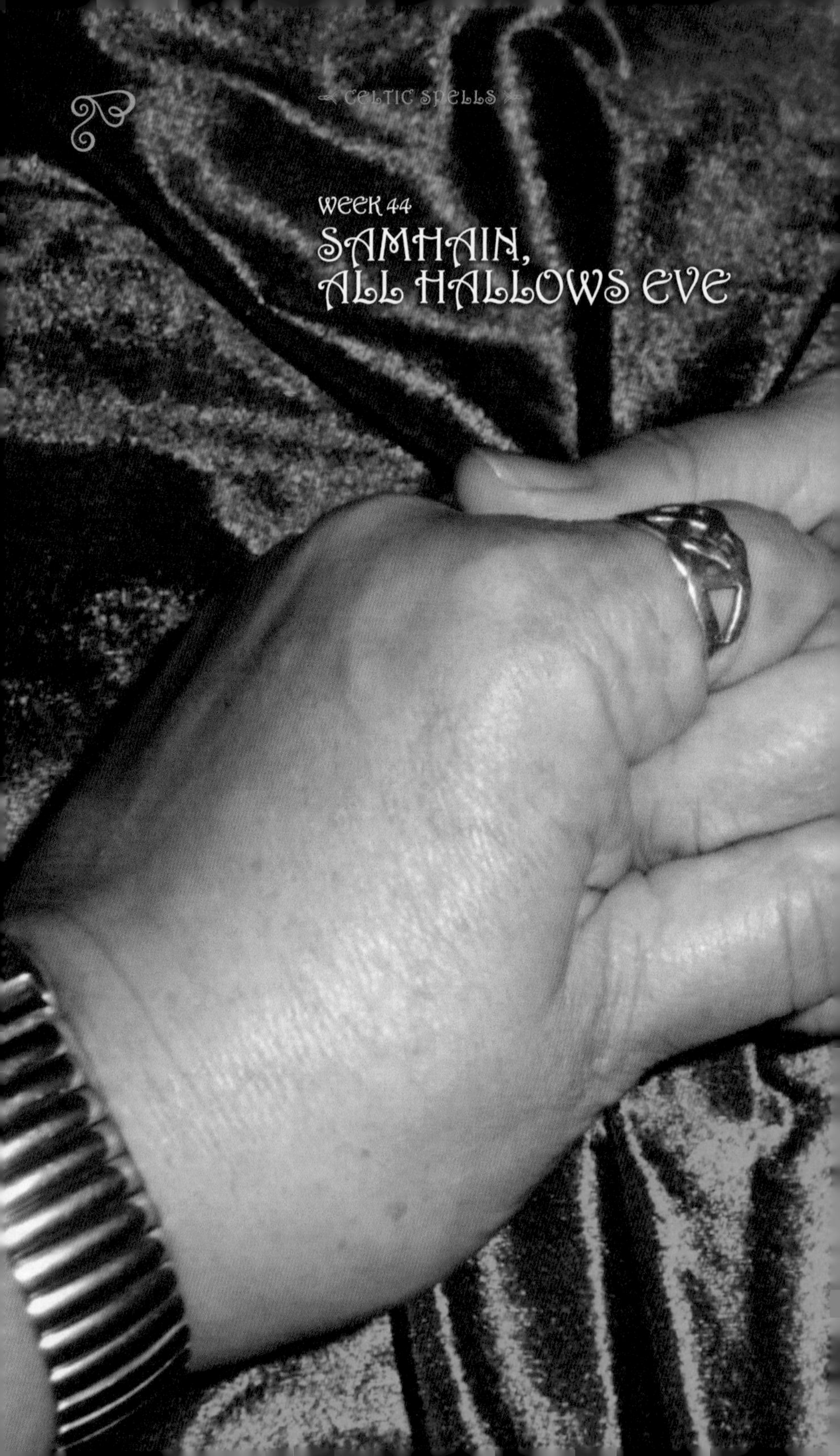

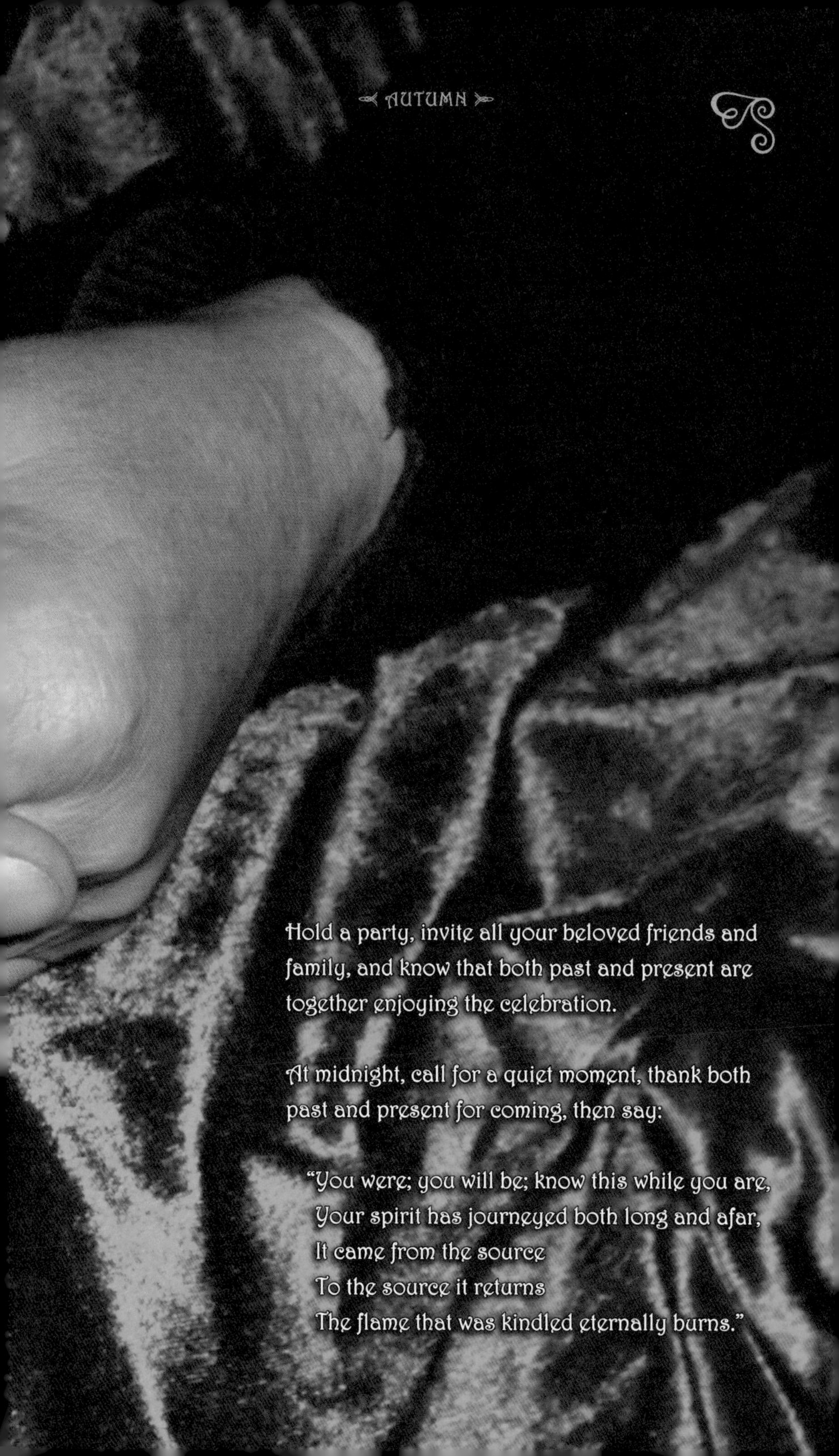

Hold a party, invite all your beloved friends and family, and know that both past and present are together enjoying the celebration.

At midnight, call for a quiet moment, thank both past and present for coming, then say:

> "You were; you will be; know this while you are,
> Your spirit has journeyed both long and afar,
> It came from the source
> To the source it returns
> The flame that was kindled eternally burns."

WINTER

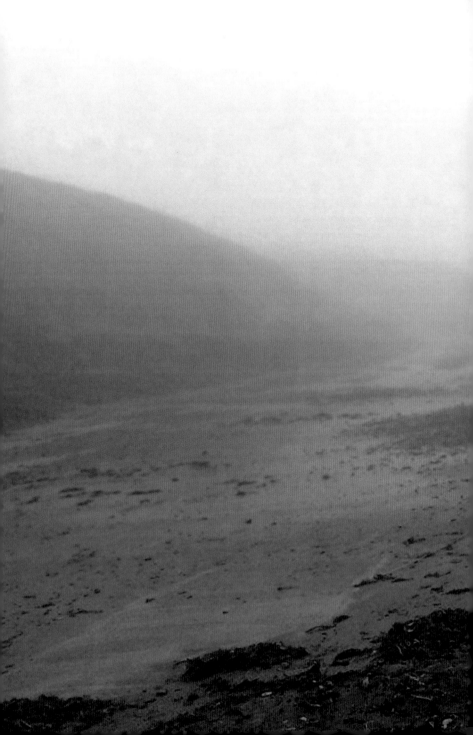

NOVEMBER

There is chill now, and dampness in the air. The landscape is bleak, with stark trees, and heavy skies turn the world a miserable brown. Nights are long and cold, a fire in the hearth is much needed. This is the perfect setting for Celtic Bardic traditional storytelling. Woolly jumpers are the code of dress and cold hands are kept warm busy creating all manner of crafting, all in preparation for Yule's much needed gifts and entertaining.

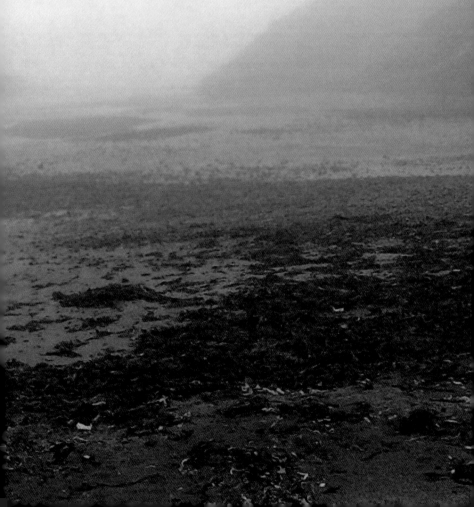

WEEK 45

BESOM SPELL

Take a besom broom and sweep your home, whether in reality or just symbolically. This spell is to remove the remnants of the old year and herald in the energies of the new. The symbolism incorporated also accounts for your own inner world, sweeping clean your emotional clutter.

While you sweep, say:

"Sweep out the old, sweep in the new
Just like Grandma used to do;
Out with dust go shadows as well,
Welcome the new; let all be well."

WEEK 46

HAZEL WISDOM

Hazel is the Celtic tree of Wisdom, Aife is the Goddess of learning.
Take three whole, unbroken hazelnuts and a tumble stone of fluorite.
Put the nuts one by one, followed by the stone,
into a small green cloth bag saying:

"Aife give power to this spell,
Help me learn to listen well,
May I understand and know
That in wisdom I might grow."

Take this amulet with you to exams and tests.

WEEK 47

ACORN PROTECTION SPELL

Collect seven (the number of protection) unspoilt acorns and put them in a small pottery bowl with a piece of red agate. As you add the acorns and stone, say seven times:

"Acorns of the oaken tree
Protect my property
Protect me."

Now stand the bowl on the windowsill by the main door.

WEEK 48

SPELL OF CHANGE

Wait for a really windy day. Climb a hill or to a high (but safe) place, stand and feel the wind buffet you, feel the power of Don, Queen of the Heavens, embrace the element of Air. Through deep breathing establish connectivity, then say three times, escalating the volume with each repetition:

"Goddess of both sky and sea,
Blow the winds of change for me
I need opportunity."

DECEMBER

Days are short and bitterly cold, the darkness of night draws in so quickly. Holly and ivy seem to be the only trees alive in woods; their hardy leaves reminding us green will return and vanquish brown.

Seasonal celebrations abound; this is a time of family reunion to catch up on the activities of the past year, so stock the pantry well in case the weather becomes restricting. And remember, Nature also needs a helping hand.

WEEK 49

WAX AND WATER DIVINATION

Place a glass bowl on the table and part-fill with water. Take a large stout candle that has been alight for a while, that has a pool of hot wax. As you tip the wax into the water say:

"Gracious Mother I would see
What the future holds for me."

Allow the hot wax to cool then lift it out and look. Read the symbolism therein.
What do you see?

WEEK 50
LOVING BREW

Make a hot stew. Using a large pot, add the ingredients and chant as you stir. The words will be your own and the list can be as long as you want. As you stir, add in positivity and take out its negative opposite.

For example chant: "I stir in happiness – I stir out sorrow."
"I stir in prosperity – I stir out poverty."

Complete the cooking, saying: "Goddess, this I ask of you,
Bless now this Loving Brew."

WEEK 51

CROSSROADS SPELL

These are long black nights and in ancient times it was easy for a traveller to get lost in the darkness and take the wrong turning at a crossroads. Nowadays this has a metaphoric meaning, for we too can easily take the wrong turning.

Bake a cake and leave it at the side of a crossroads, saying:

"Goddess of the night,
Give light to those who stray.
Show them the way."

WEEK 52

DON'T FORGET THE ROBIN

Now is the time to choose and dress an exterior Yule Tree, a Goddess, one that will help the birds.

On a tree outside, leave your gifts for the children of the Mother, wish them a Merry Christmas 'for in giving we receive'. As you work, say:

"Yule blessing to you my little friends,
Stay warm and well 'til winter ends
And the Sun returns."

7555538R00055

Printed in Great Britain
by Amazon.co.uk, Ltd.,
Marston Gate.